# Horse
## & Pony Breeds

WRITTEN BY
Sandy Ransford

PHOTOGRAPHED BY
Bob Langrish

KINGFISHER

KINGFISHER

Kingfisher Publications Plc
New Penderel House
283–288 High Holborn
London WC1V 7HZ

www.kingfisherpub.com

First published by
Kingfisher Publications Plc 2003

10 9 8 7 6 5 4 3 2 1

1TR/0103/TWP/CLSN(CLSN)/150ENSOMA

ISBN 0 7534 0826 0

**Designed and edited by:**
Picthall & Gunzi Ltd

Editor: Lauren Robertson
Designer: Dominic Zwemmer
DTP Assistant: Anthony Cutting
Editorial Assistant: Carmen Hansen
Editorial Director: Christiane Gunzi

**Additional photography by**:
Houghtons Horses p21br, p22b, p27tl,
p36bl, p40br, p44bl, p46br, p46bl, p50bl,
p51c, p59tr; Only Horses Picture
Library p26bl, p33b, p35bl, p55b

**For Kingfisher:**
Editorial Director: Miranda Smith
Art Director: Mike Davis
DTP Manager: Nicky Studdart

Printed in Singapore

# Contents

# What is a breed?

**H**orses and ponies vary in shape and size. Some belong to a particular breed. This means that they share the same characteristics as other horses or ponies of the same breed.

Horse breeds are divided into groups called coldblood, hotblood and warmblood. The pony breeds are not usually classified in this way.

## Coldbloods

Brabants (above) are typical coldblood horses. Coldbloods come from northern Europe, where the cool, damp weather produces plenty of rich grazing. This makes the horses bred there large and very strong.

## Warmbloods

Warmblood breeds were produced by crossing hotbloods and coldbloods. This horse (left) is a warmblood, although it does not belong to a specific breed. It is a 'type' called a heavyweight hunter. Types of horse are defined by the kind of work they do.

## Hotbloods

The Anglo-Arab (above) is a fine example of the beauty, grace and elegance of the hotblood breeds. Hotbloods originally came from the Middle East and North Africa, where poor grazing and the extreme climate produced a light, tough, fast horse.

## Ponies

Ponies stand up to 14.2hh (147cm) and most, like the Icelandics (right), are warmbloods. Ponies have shorter legs than horses, and they are stronger in relation to their size. They are sturdy, tough and independent.

# Types of horse

Horses and ponies vary in type from the large, heavily built, slow-moving draught horse to the slender, fast Thoroughbred; from the solid, weight-carrying cob to the elegant show pony. Types are usually a mixture of different breeds, though many are specially bred. For example, a heavy horse crossed with a Thoroughbred will produce a horse capable of carrying a large, heavy rider.

## Driving types

Horses and ponies suitable for driving tend to have straight shoulders – on which the collar of the harness fits well – and upright pasterns. They often have high action, which looks good when they are pulling a carriage, but would be very uncomfortable in a riding horse.

**Heavy horses**
This type of horse is massively built. Their bones are huge and they have enormous muscles. They are capable of pulling very heavy weights.

**Carriage horses**
These types must also be strong, but they are lighter, more elegantly built, and often high-stepping. A matching pair is highly prized.

## Riding types

A riding horse or pony has to be strong enough to carry its rider, but narrow enough to ride. Sloping shoulders give a horse a long, low stride, which is comfortable to sit to. Sloping pasterns also make a horse a good ride, while powerful hindquarters and long hind legs give jumping ability.

**Show pony**
A show pony or the larger version, called a show hack, has all the best points of a riding pony or horse. It must be beautiful, have good conformation and paces, and behave perfectly.

### Cob
A cob is a quiet riding horse, with short legs and a deep body. Traditionally it was ridden by elderly, often heavy, riders. A cob's mane is usually hogged.

### Polo ponies
These are actually small horses. They have to be fast, able to start, stop and turn quickly, and must obey their riders' commands instantly.

### Working hunter pony
This is more solidly built and plainer than the classic show pony. As well as being a good general riding pony, it must be able to gallop and jump.

# Colours

The colour of a horse's or pony's coat depends on the amount of pigment, or natural colouring, in its skin. Almost all horses and ponies have dark skin, except where they have white markings, such as on the face and lower legs, where the skin is pink. Only rare, pure-white horses called albinos have pink skin all over. Most horses and ponies that we think of as white are actually grey. They have dark skin, which you can see on their muzzles.

## As horses age

As horses and ponies grow older, their colour may change. Greys are born dark and gradually become lighter, until they look white. Some greys develop dark, usually brown, flecks. This colour is called 'flea-bitten grey'. Browns, blacks, bays and chestnuts may have some white hairs in their coats, manes and tails.

**Bay** is a rich, reddish-brown coat colour with black mane, tail and lower legs.

**Flea-bitten grey** is a light grey colour with dark, usually brown, flecks.

**Bright bay** is lighter than bay, with more yellow in the coat colour.

**Brown** is dark brown, often with paler areas. Also called dark bay.

**Dapple grey** has black and white hairs that form rings called dapples.

**Black** is black all over, including the mane and tail. Pure black is rare.

# Eye colour

The colour of a horse's or pony's eyes, like that of its coat, is decided by the amount of pigment it has. As most horses and ponies have dark skin, so most also have brown eyes. But occasionally, as with the albino, and sometimes with spotted horses, the eyes are light coloured. In the Appaloosa breed, the white of the eye can be seen all the time.

 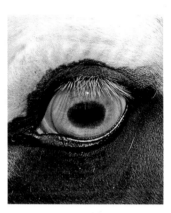

**Brown eyes**
The iris of the eye is dark brown. The white of the eye, which surrounds the iris, can be seen only when the horse is frightened or angry.

**Wall eyes**
In a wall eye, the iris is bluish- or pinkish-white. This unusual colour does not affect the horse's sight. These are also called china, blue or glass eyes.

# Hoof colour

The colour of the horn of a horse's or pony's hooves is related to the colour of its coat on the leg just above the hoof. Black or dark-coloured legs have dark hooves, which are called blue. Where there are white socks or other leg markings, the hooves are light-coloured, and are called white. A horse may have hooves that are different colours.

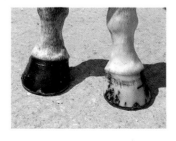 

**Blue hoof and white hoof**
The pony's leg shown on the left of the picture is dark and has a blue hoof. The leg on the right has a white sock, so the hoof is also white.

**Striped hooves**
Horse and pony breeds with spotted coats, such as the Appaloosa, have striped hooves (above). Light and dark stripes run up and down the feet.

**Liver chestnut** is a darker chestnut, like the colour of raw liver.

**Chestnut** is red-gold or ginger, often with darker or lighter mane and tail.

**Blue roan** is black with white growing through it, giving a bluish colour.

**Strawberry roan** is chestnut with white hairs growing through it.

**Yellow dun** is a yellowish, biscuit-coloured coat with black points.

**Skewbald** is brown and white patches all over. Also called part-coloured.

**Piebald** is black and white patches all over. Also called part-coloured.

**Spotted** is dark spots on a white coat or white spots on a dark coat.

# Markings

The word 'markings' means all the patches and stripes on a horse or pony that are a different colour from its coat. These markings are usually white and appear on the face and legs. The shape and size of the markings varies a lot between different horses, and they are recorded, and used to help to identify the animal.

## Face markings

Marks on the face are white and usually appear on the front of the face. These marks may cover a large area or a very small one, and can be of many different shapes. To make it easier to describe these marks and record them, different types of markings are given special names.

**Blaze** is a fairly broad white band down the face.

## Flesh marks

White patches on the underside of a horse's belly and on its flanks are called 'flesh marks'. These marks are often seen on Clydesdale horses (left). Sometimes, horses have white marks on their backs or in other places. These are usually the result of an injury or wound, and are called 'acquired marks'.

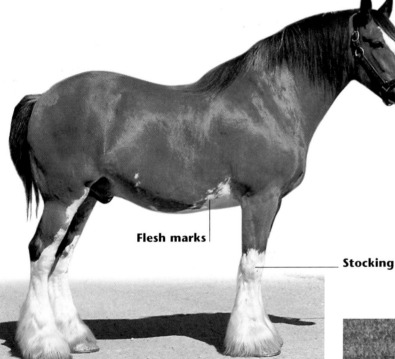

Blaze

Flesh marks

Stocking

## Leg markings

Leg markings are mostly white and are usually called socks or stockings, but there may also be dark marks. When markings are written down to help to identify a horse, they are described very carefully. For example, a certificate may say 'white mid-pastern to coronet' or 'white to mid-cannon'.

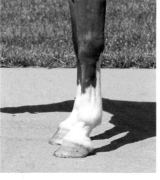

**Socks** are white marks that go above the fetlock but not as far as the knee or hock.

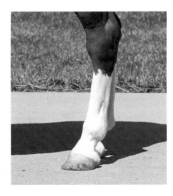

**Stockings** are white marks that reach and sometimes cover the knee or hock.

**Stripe** is a narrow band of white down the face.

**Star** is a white mark of any shape on the forehead.

**Snip** is a patch of white on the nose between the nostrils.

**Whorl** is a ring of hair that grows in different directions.

# Eel stripe

Primitive breeds, such as Przewalski's Horse (right), and Fjord and Highland ponies often have a black stripe running along their backs from the mane to the tail. This is called an 'eel' or 'dorsal' stripe, and is usually seen with a dun-coloured coat.

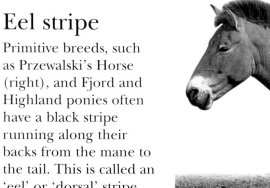

**Eel stripe**

# White face

A very broad white blaze that goes all the way across the front of a horse's face is called a 'white face'. It reaches as far as the eyes and covers the horse's muzzle.

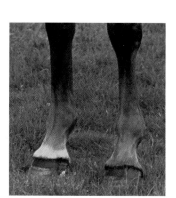

**White coronets** cover the area just above the hoof, which is called the coronet.

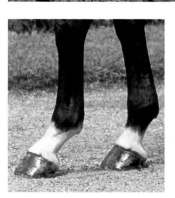

**White pasterns** cover the pastern area between the hoof and the fetlock joint.

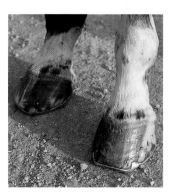

**Ermine marks** are small dark spots on white socks next to dark marks on the hooves.

**Zebra marks** are horizontal dark stripes on the lower legs seen in ancient breeds.

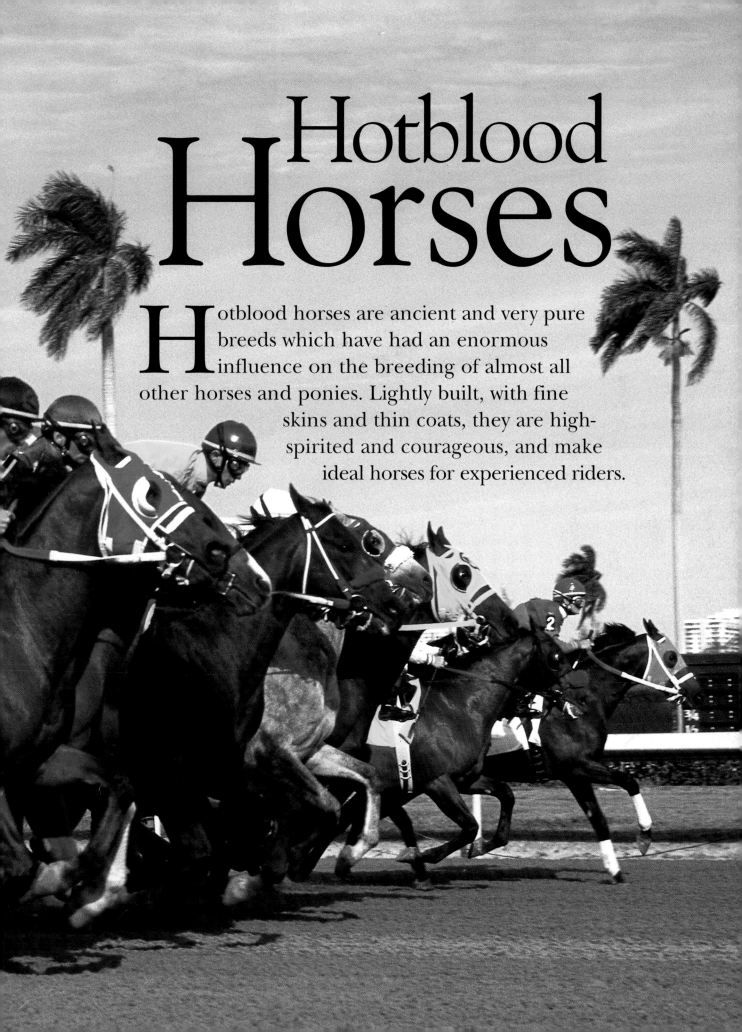

# Hotblood Horses

**H**otblood horses are ancient and very pure breeds which have had an enormous influence on the breeding of almost all other horses and ponies. Lightly built, with fine skins and thin coats, they are high-spirited and courageous, and make ideal horses for experienced riders.

# Arab

The Arab is probably the oldest and most beautiful breed of horse in the world. It has played an important part in the development of horse and pony breeds in almost every country. With its high head and tail carriage, great 'presence' and floating action, an Arabian horse is instantly recognizable. Although it is a small horse, the Arab is strong, and famous for its stamina.

## Arabian head

The head is small and elegant, with a 'dished', or concave, profile. The neck has a high crest. The angle at which the neck joins the head, called the *mitbah*, is seen only in this breed.

An Arab's back is short and compact because it has fewer bones in its spine than other horses. The joints of the legs are flat and the pasterns are sloping. The chest is broad, and the feet are hard and well-formed.

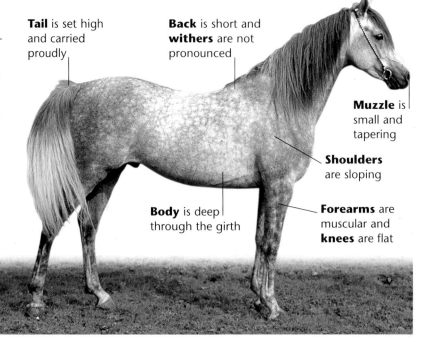

**Tail** is set high and carried proudly

**Back** is short and **withers** are not pronounced

**Muzzle** is small and tapering

**Shoulders** are sloping

**Body** is deep through the girth

**Forearms** are muscular and **knees** are flat

**Mare and foal**
An Arabian horse is high-spirited and courageous, but it also has a kind and gentle nature which makes it easy to handle. Arab foals are lively and inquisitive.

## Desert horses

Arabs were first bred in the deserts of the Arabian peninsula, where they have existed for at least 4,000 years. Poor food and harsh conditions have produced a small, fast horse that is strong and tough. They were raced over more than 450km, and regarded as prized possessions by their owners.

## Facts and figures

- **Place of origin**
  The Arabian peninsula,
  now called Saudi Arabia

- **Height**
  14.2–15hh (147–152cm),
  or larger

- **Colour**
  Mostly chestnut, bay and
  grey; brown and black
  are seen rarely

- **Uses**
  General riding; showing;
  endurance riding;
  specialist racing; also as a
  cross with other breeds
  to produce quality show
  hacks and ponies

- **Characteristics**
  Courageous and gentle

# Thoroughbred

The Thoroughbred is the fastest breed of horse in the world. It was produced in England in the 17th and 18th centuries by crossing three Arab stallions – the Darley Arabian, the Godolphin Arabian and the Byerley Turk – with English mares. Thoroughbreds have developed into perfect racehorses. They have also had a huge effect on horse breeding throughout the world. They succeed at all kinds of equestrian sports, and make good riding horses.

## Thoroughbred breeding

Thoroughbred horses are very valuable. Those to be used for racing are called bloodstock, and are bred from former racehorses on special stud farms. Young horses are turned out together in paddocks until they are old enough to begin their training.

## On the gallops

When Thoroughbred racehorses have become used to carrying a rider and obeying commands, they are trained on stretches of land called gallops. Here they can gallop for long distances. They usually exercise in groups, called strings, supervised by their trainers.

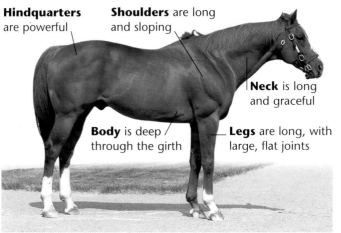

**Hindquarters** are powerful

**Shoulders** are long and sloping

**Neck** is long and graceful

**Body** is deep through the girth

**Legs** are long, with large, flat joints

## Steeplechasing

Thoroughbreds compete in both flat racing and racing over fences, which is called 'steeplechasing'. The grey above right is Desert Orchid, one of the most successful of recent steeplechasers. He is shown here racing at Cheltenham, England, in 1990.

**Eventing**
Many horses that compete in eventing are either pure- or part-bred Thoroughbreds.

Many people believe that this breed is the perfect riding horse. Its sloping shoulders and long pasterns produce long, low strides, making it comfortable to ride. Its powerful quarters give it great speed. It is light and graceful, yet strong, and has great stamina.

## Facts and figures

- **Place of origin**
  England

- **Height**
  15.2–16.2hh
  (157–168cm)

- **Colour**
  Brown, bay,
  chestnut, grey
  Always solid colours

- **Uses**
  Racing; riding;
  showing; dressage;
  showjumping;
  eventing

- **Characteristics**
  Fast, courageous,
  but also highly
  strung and can be
  difficult to handle

# Anglo-Arab

**Withers** are higher than Arab's

**Quarters** are strong

**Head** has Arab's gentle expression

**Legs** have plenty of bone

**Body** is deep through the girth

The Anglo-Arab is a cross between the Arab and the Thoroughbred. It has the beauty and intelligence of the Arab, and the size and speed of the Thoroughbred. Although the breed originated in England, much of its development took place in France.

## Endurance riding

Anglo-Arabs, as well as pure-bred and part-bred Arabs, compete very successfully in long-distance endurance rides. The horses must be extremely fit and have great stamina, as they may have to travel up to 80km a day at an average speed of 14–15km/h. Some endurance rides last for more than one day.

The head is straighter in profile than the Arab's, and the horse looks more like a Thoroughbred because of its greater size. Its long legs enable it to move with great speed. Its size means that it does very well in eventing and showjumping, as well as in dressage.

### Key facts
- **Height**
  15.2–16.2hh
  (157–168cm)

- **Colour**
  Bay, chestnut,
  brown, grey

- **Uses**
  Riding; endurance;
  dressage; showjumping

# Barb

The Barb comes from Morocco, in North Africa, and is one of the world's oldest breeds. Although it is not beautiful, the Barb is sound and tough, and has great stamina. It is capable of great speed over short distances.

Mane and tail are thick and full

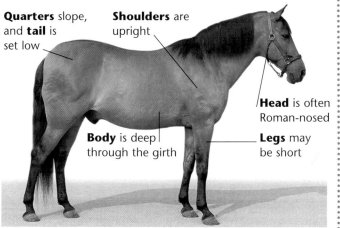

Quarters slope, and tail is set low

Shoulders are upright

Head is often Roman-nosed

Body is deep through the girth

Legs may be short

## Head shape

The Barb is such an ancient breed that its skull shape is similar to that of primitive horses. The head is quite large and plain and does not have the Arab's grace and beauty.

The Barb, like the Arab, has had a great influence on horse breeding throughout the world. The Spanish Horse, from which many horse and pony breeds were developed, was itself descended from the Barb. The breed is the traditional mount of the Berbers of North Africa.

# Akhal-Teké

Bred in the deserts of Turkmenistan, north of Iran, the Akhal-Teké is an unusual-looking horse. It has a long, lean body and neck, and long legs. It is capable of great feats of endurance, and is used for long-distance riding, racing, jumping and dressage.

The Akhal-Teké has been bred for thousands of years. It is spirited and courageous, hardy and strong. This breed stands about 15.2hh (157cm) and has a fine coat and a silky mane and tail. The most prized colour is this unique metallic golden dun.

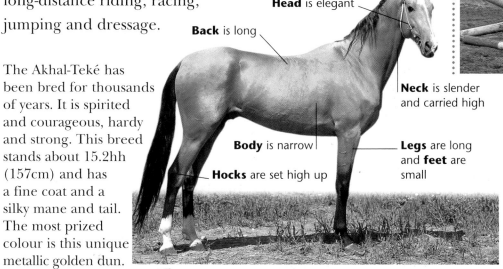

Head is elegant

Back is long

Neck is slender and carried high

Body is narrow

Legs are long and feet are small

Hocks are set high up

## Good jumper

Because of its great stamina, the Akhal-Teké is mainly known for its success in long-distance riding and racing. But it is also a good jumper, and competes successfully in both showjumping and dressage.

# Coldblood Horses

Coldblood breeds are large, heavy and very strong. Many have existed for thousands of years. They were bred for farm work and for pulling heavy loads. Coldbloods have calm and docile natures. Most have 'feather' – hair – round their feet.

# Ardennais

This heavy draught horse has been bred in the Ardennes region, on the borders of France and Belgium, for hundreds of years. It is probably descended from medieval warhorses. In the 19th century, the Ardennais developed into two main types – a massive farm horse and a more lightweight animal.

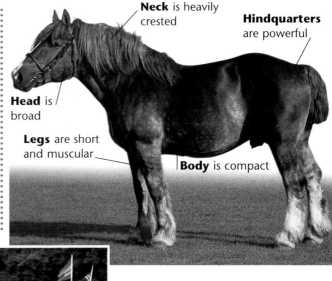

**Neck** is heavily crested

**Hindquarters** are powerful

**Head** is broad

**Legs** are short and muscular

**Body** is compact

## Crowd-pullers

Ardennais are not often used for farming today, but these good-natured, easy-to-handle horses are still popular at shows. This pair, pulling a farm wagon, are the typical red roan colour.

Ardennais stand between 15 and 16hh (152–163cm). They are tough, hardy animals, able to withstand a harsh climate and do well on poor food. Ardennais horses are often roan in colour, although they may also be bay, chestnut or grey.

**Hindquarters** are very muscular

**Neck** has a massive crest and a fine, silky mane

**Head** is elegant

**Shoulders** are powerful

**Legs** are huge and carry little feather

# Boulonnais

The Boulonnais comes from the area round Boulogne, in northeast France. Two types of Boulonnais were bred – one was a heavy farm worker and the other was a lighter, faster horse called a *mareyeur* (meaning 'fish-seller'). This horse was used for transporting fish from the coast to Paris.

Despite its size, the Boulonnais is an elegant horse due to its Arab and Barb ancestors. It is usually grey, but also sometimes black, roan, bay or chestnut. This horse is well proportioned, and has a fine coat and thick, silky mane and tail hair. It stands between 16 and 17hh (163–173cm).

## Fast action

The Boulonnais can move faster than most heavy horses and has lower knee action. Some still work on farms, but to ensure the breed does not die out, the French government breeds Boulonnais.

# Percheron

This powerful breed comes from La Perche in northern France. Its ancestors carried knights who wore heavy armour. In the 18th century, the Percheron was crossed with Arabs, giving it greater quality and better action. The horses are clean-legged, a great advantage when they worked on the land.

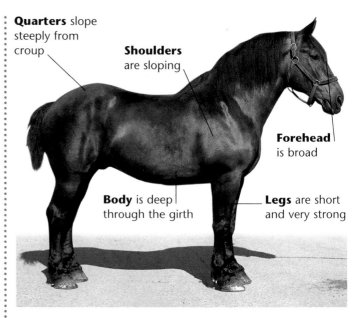

**Quarters** slope steeply from croup

**Shoulders** are sloping

**Forehead** is broad

**Body** is deep through the girth

**Legs** are short and very strong

## Facts and figures

- **Place of origin**
  Normandy, France
- **Height**
  16.1–17.2hh (165–178cm)
- **Colour**
  Grey or black
- **Uses**
  Farm work; coaching

One of the tallest horses that has ever lived was a Percheron. It stood 21hh (213cm), though not many of them are as large as that. Percherons are broad, compact and very strong with sturdy legs and good feet. The breed has a more elegant appearance, lower action and a finer head than most heavy breeds because of its Arab blood.

### Carriage horses

Although some Percherons still work on the land, they are also popular as carriage horses. Despite being so large, they have a low, free action and move easily. They are docile and work well.

# Suffolk

Often called the Suffolk Punch, this is the most pure-bred of all Britain's heavy horses. All Suffolks are descended from one stallion called the Horse of Ufford, which was born in 1768. The Suffolk is stocky with short legs, and is always chestnut in colour. Some Suffolks are used for farm work, but the breed is now mostly seen in the show ring.

**Suffolk foal**
Suffolks mature early and live for a long time. This foal may start its working life at two years old, and continue for many years. Suffolks are valuable as both farm horses and draught horses in towns.

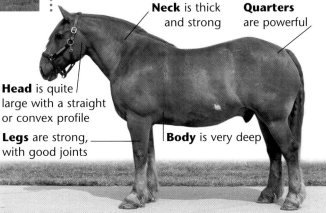

**Neck** is thick and strong

**Quarters** are powerful

**Head** is quite large with a straight or convex profile

**Legs** are strong, with good joints

**Body** is very deep

The Suffolk has a round, barrel-shaped body on short, strong legs. Its chest is wide, and it has a thick neck with low withers. Despite its bulk, the horse moves freely and has an energetic trot. It has a friendly and docile temperament, and is easy to handle.

## Key facts

- **Place of origin**
  Suffolk, England

- **Height**
  16–16.3hh
  (163–170cm)

- **Colour**
  Always chestnut, with no white markings except on the face

## Farm horse

The Suffolk was bred to work on farms in eastern England. The lack of feather on its legs is an advantage, as it means that the heavy clay soil does not cling to them. Suffolks do not need a lot of food, which makes them cheap to keep.

# Shire

Tall and extremely strong, the Shire is probably the heaviest of England's heavy horses. It can weigh up to 1,219kg and may stand up to 17.2hh (178cm). Some are even taller. Its girth can measure up to 2.4m. The Shire gets its name from the English counties where it was bred (Derbyshire, Staffordshire, Lincolnshire and Leicestershire). Shire horses often worked on farms. Many brewers also used them to pull carts called drays to deliver beer in cities.

## Knights' horse

In medieval times, the Shire was called 'the great horse of England'. Its size and strength made it the ideal horse for carrying knights in armour, who could weigh up to 190kg. This breed was also an all-round workhorse, employed on farms and wherever great pulling power was needed.

## Ploughing match

There are not many working Shire horses today, but they are often seen at ploughing matches and shows. Their manes are braided and plumed, and their bridles and harness gleam with polished brasses. They are a magnificent sight, and their strength and gentleness are much admired.

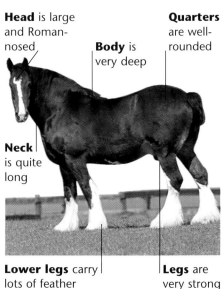

**Head** is large and Roman-nosed

**Body** is very deep

**Quarters** are well-rounded

**Neck** is quite long

**Lower legs** carry lots of feather

**Legs** are very strong

This tall and extremely powerful horse is able to pull five times its own weight. A Shire is usually black, bay, brown or grey in colour. Its legs often have long white stockings, and the feather is fine and silky. Shires' tails are often cut short, which means that they lose their natural fly whisks.

**Kindly horse**
The Shire has a broad forehead. The large eyes have a kindly expression, which shows how gentle this breed can be. The face often has a broad white blaze that goes over the nose and the muzzle.

**Neck** is thick and arched

## Facts and figures

- **Place of origin**
  English Midlands

- **Height**
  16.2–17.2hh (168–178cm)

- **Colour**
  Bay, brown, black or grey

- **Uses**
  As dray horses; for showing

# Clydesdale

The Clydesdale is related to the Shire, but is lighter in build. This breed comes from Scotland, where it was originally used for farm work. Later it was used to pull various forms of transport, including coal wagons. Today, the Clydesdale is seen at shows and in ploughing matches. It is also crossed with Thoroughbreds to produce heavyweight riding horses.

Clydesdales are usually bay, brown, black or roan. They often have white markings that start at their feet and go right up the legs. Some cover part of the horse's belly, and the face may be mostly white, too. These big horses stand about 16.2 to 17hh (168–173cm).

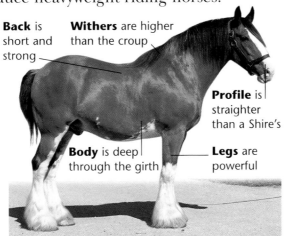

**Back** is short and strong

**Withers** are higher than the croup

**Profile** is straighter than a Shire's

**Body** is deep through the girth

**Legs** are powerful

**Trade turnout**
Beautifully decorated Clydesdales are often seen at shows, harnessed to brightly painted vehicles called trade turnouts.

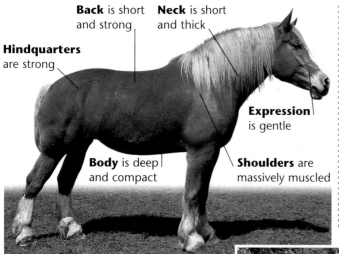

**Back** is short and strong

**Neck** is short and thick

**Hindquarters** are strong

**Expression** is gentle

**Body** is deep and compact

**Shoulders** are massively muscled

# Brabant

This ancient breed dates back to Roman times and is also known as the Brabançon and Belgian Heavy Draught. The Brabant's ancestors were warhorses, and they helped create the Shire, Clydesdale and possibly the Suffolk. The breeding of Brabants was carefully controlled to produce an impressive horse.

Standing 16 to 17hh (163 to 173cm), the Brabant is a compact, very strong horse. It is usually chestnut or red roan in colour. This breed of horse is good-natured and intelligent. It is a popular breed in the United States, as well as in its native Belgium.

## Still working

The Brabant is not used much for farm work nowadays, but can still be seen working in harness. This pair is pulling a bus through the streets of a small, European-style town in California.

# Noriker

This Austrian breed dates back to the 16th century. Its name comes from the word 'Noricum', which was a Roman province situated where Austria is now. The Noriker is related to the Haflinger, and was bred to work on the farms and forests of the Austrian Alps. It is strong, hard-working and easy to handle.

**Mane** and **tail** are often flaxen

**Back** is long

**Nostrils** are wide

**Legs** are strong and carry little feather

**Girth** is massive

## Broad horse

The Noriker has a broad chest, and its girth measurement should not be less than 60 per cent of its height. It has short, sturdy legs. This breed's tough constitution helps it to withstand the harsh Alpine winters.

The Noriker stands between 16 and 17hh (163–173cm) and is chestnut, brown or black in colour. The legs are strong, and its action is longer and lower than that of many heavy breeds. It has a calm temperament, is sure-footed and economical to keep.

# Friesian

This attractive breed from the Netherlands was the mount of German and Friesian knights during the Crusades. It was used for farm work, and in the 19th century, for trotting races. Friesians are still ridden sometimes, but they are used mostly as carriage horses. As they are black, they are often used for funerals.

**Neck** is arched and carried high

**Quarters** slope from croup

**Expression** is alert

**Legs** are quite long and well-feathered

**Body** is not very deep

## Four-in-hand

Friesians are popular driving horses. They look very smart and they have a fast, high-stepping trot. This team, called a four-in-hand, is owned by Harrods, London's famous department store.

Standing between 15 and 16hh (152–163cm), the Friesian is black all over, though some may have a small white star on their foreheads. The horse is lighter in build than many heavy breeds. The Friesian has a good temperament and is easy to handle.

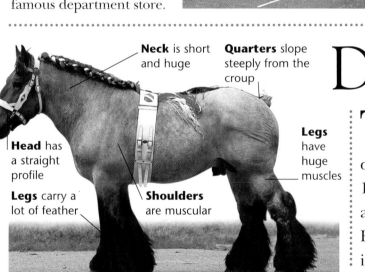

**Neck** is short and huge

**Quarters** slope steeply from the croup

**Head** has a straight profile

**Legs** have huge muscles

**Legs** carry a lot of feather

**Shoulders** are muscular

# Dutch Draught

This breed is believed to be the most massively built of all European heavy draught horses. It was developed in the late 19th and early 20th centuries from Ardennais and native horses. The Royal Dutch Draught Horse Society controls its breeding. The result is a very heavy and powerful working horse.

## Show horse

Today, Dutch Draughts are mostly seen in the show ring, where they may be driven to a variety of carts. Some, however, are still used to pull vehicles around city streets, selling or advertizing goods.

The Dutch Draught stands about 16.3hh (170cm) and is usually chestnut, bay, roan, grey or black in colour. Although it is very heavy, its action is free and active. This breed matures early and is long-lived. The Dutch Draught has a quiet nature and is a good worker.

# Warmblood Horses

**M**ost of the horse and pony breeds throughout the world are classed as 'warmbloods'. Many types of horses and ponies also belong to this group. Warmblood horses include the highly successful German and Dutch competition horses, and most of the American breeds.

# Swedish Warmblood

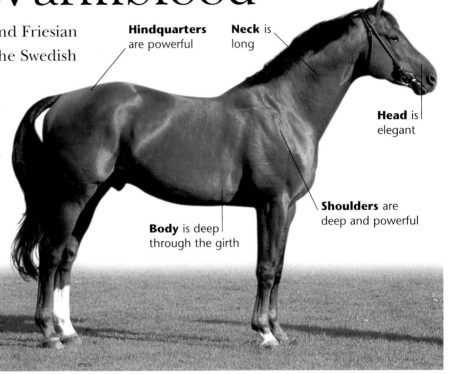

**Hindquarters** are powerful

**Neck** is long

**Head** is elegant

**Shoulders** are deep and powerful

**Body** is deep through the girth

Bred from Spanish, oriental and Friesian horses in the 17th century, the Swedish Warmblood was a cavalry horse. Later, the breed was crossed with Thoroughbreds, Trakehners, Hanoverians and Arabs. Today, it is a competition horse, good at jumping, eventing and dressage.

Standing around 16.2 to 17hh (168–173cm), the Swedish Warmblood is a big, athletic horse. It has powerful shoulders and quarters, strong legs and good feet. Its calm temperament and sensible attitude help make it good at dressage. It can be any solid colour.

# Selle Français

The Selle Français (meaning 'French saddle') was bred in Normandy, France, in the 19th century, from native Norman horses and imported English Thoroughbreds. In the middle of the 20th century, French Trotters, Thoroughbreds, Arabs and Anglo-Arabs were used to develop the breed.

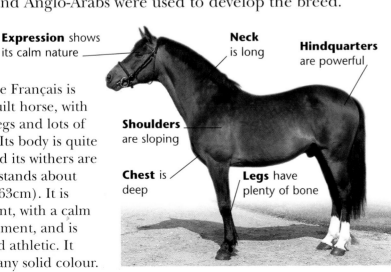

**Expression** shows its calm nature

**Neck** is long

**Hindquarters** are powerful

**Shoulders** are sloping

**Chest** is deep

**Legs** have plenty of bone

The Selle Français is a well-built horse, with strong legs and lots of muscle. Its body is quite long, and its withers are high. It stands about 16hh (163cm). It is intelligent, with a calm temperament, and is agile and athletic. It may be any solid colour.

## Good jumper

This horse excels at showjumping and eventing. It tackles difficult cross-country fences bravely, and is good at dressage. It makes a good all-round riding horse. In France, some Selle Français are bred especially for racing.

# Competition breeds

Although many breeds and types of horse are good at dressage, eventing and showjumping, the breeds described here are particularly well known for it. They were produced by crossing farm and carriage horses with English Thoroughbreds. This made lighter, faster horses, which kept the calmer nature of the heavier animals.

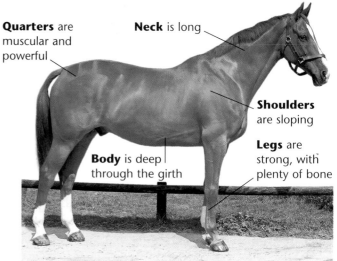

**Quarters** are muscular and powerful

**Neck** is long

**Shoulders** are sloping

**Legs** are strong, with plenty of bone

**Body** is deep through the girth

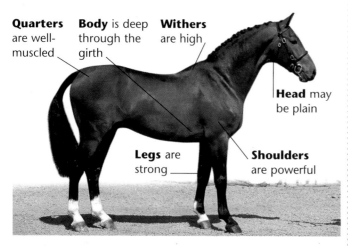

**Quarters** are well-muscled

**Body** is deep through the girth

**Withers** are high

**Head** may be plain

**Legs** are strong

**Shoulders** are powerful

## Hanoverian

This breed was developed in the 18th century by crossing Holsteins with local mares. This produced a strong horse that was used for farm work. Trakehners and English Thoroughbreds were used to improve the breed and create a first-class competition horse.

## Dutch Warmblood

This breed was created in the 20th century by crossing the Gelderlander and the Groningen with the English Thoroughbred. It is possibly the most successful of the competition breeds. These horses are strong and athletic, with a calm temperament.

**Dressage champion**
Strong, athletic and with good action, this breed is superb at dressage. This picture shows Isabell Werth on Nissan Gigolo riding for Germany.

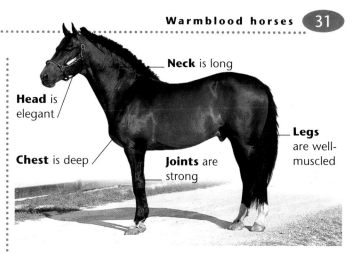

Neck is long

Head is elegant

Chest is deep

Joints are strong

Legs are well-muscled

**Famous partnership**
One of the most famous dressage partnerships of all time was Jennie Loriston-Clarke and Dutch Courage, here giving a demonstration of long-reining.

# Holstein

Between the 17th and 19th centuries, Holsteins were used as carriage horses. Since the 19th century, they have been bred for riding. They are excellent at cross-country, and do well in dressage and showjumping.

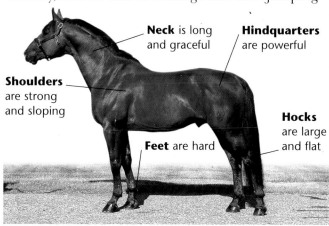

Neck is long and graceful

Hindquarters are powerful

Shoulders are strong and sloping

Hocks are large and flat

Feet are hard

Marius, the highly successful Dutch Warmblood stallion, jumping in Calgary, Canada, in 1979.

# Trakehner

This breed began in East Prussia in the 13th century. Originally a carriage horse, it was crossed with Arabs and Thoroughbreds to produce cavalry horses. It is a first-class dressage, jumping and eventing competitor.

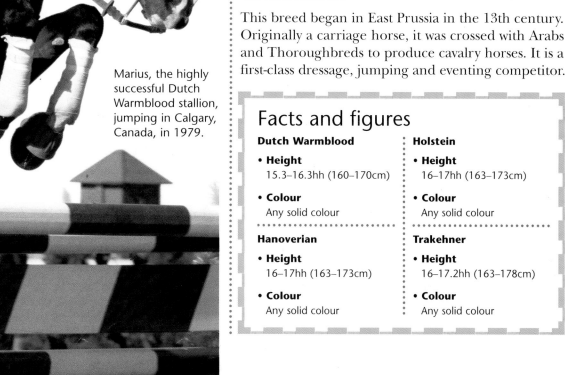

## Facts and figures

**Dutch Warmblood**
- **Height**
  15.3–16.3hh (160–170cm)
- **Colour**
  Any solid colour

**Hanoverian**
- **Height**
  16–17hh (163–173cm)
- **Colour**
  Any solid colour

**Holstein**
- **Height**
  16–17hh (163–173cm)
- **Colour**
  Any solid colour

**Trakehner**
- **Height**
  16–17.2hh (163–178cm)
- **Colour**
  Any solid colour

# Oldenburg

The tallest and heaviest of the German warmblood breeds, the Oldenburg was bred in the 17th century as a coach horse. It was named after the area of Germany from which it came, and the man who bred it, Count Anton von Oldenburg. Its ancestors include Friesian, Neapolitan, Spanish, Cleveland Bay, English Thoroughbred and Norfolk Roadster horses. Today, it is used for driving, dressage and showjumping.

The Oldenburg is a large, powerfully built horse which is between 16.2 and 17.2hh (168–178cm). It is usually bay, brown or black. It is good-natured, and matures early, giving it a long working life.

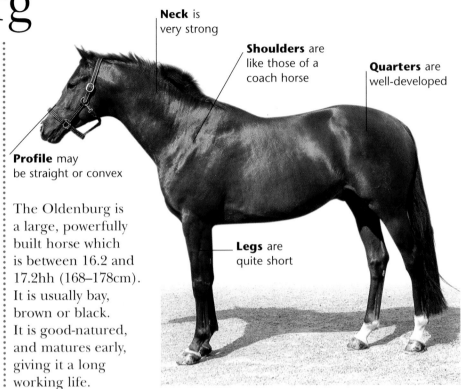

**Neck** is very strong

**Shoulders** are like those of a coach horse

**Quarters** are well-developed

**Profile** may be straight or convex

**Legs** are quite short

# Gelderlander

This breed comes from the Gelder area of the Netherlands, where it has been bred since the 19th century. Gelderlanders were then used mainly as carriage horses, but they were also expected to do light farm work and double as riding horses. Their ancestors include the Oldenburg and the Thoroughbred.

The heavily built Gelderlander stands 15.2 to 16.2hh (157–168cm), and is usually chestnut in colour. It often has a wide white blaze on its face and white stockings on its legs. Although it is not thought of as a beautiful horse, it is very strong. The Gelderlander has a gentle, docile temperament, making it easy to handle.

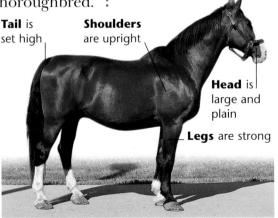

**Tail** is set high

**Shoulders** are upright

**Head** is large and plain

**Legs** are strong

## Carriage horses

Although Gelderlanders are no longer used for farm work, they are still popular carriage horses, and are used in driving competitions. They are also useful heavyweight riding horses, due to their size and strong build. These horses are not fast, but they are good jumpers.

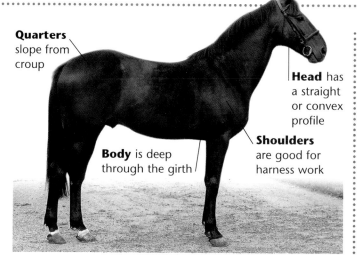

**Quarters** slope from croup

**Head** has a straight or convex profile

**Body** is deep through the girth

**Shoulders** are good for harness work

# French Trotter

This breed was developed in Normandy, France, in the 19th century, to compete in the new sport of trotting. The first trotting racecourse in France was opened in Cherbourg in 1836. The French Trotter's ancestors were the Norfolk Trotter, the English Thoroughbred and horses from the Normandy region.

The French Trotter is about 16.2hh (168cm). It may be any solid colour, but is usually bay, brown or chestnut. Strong and tough, with long legs, these horses have free-striding, active action, great stamina and are willing workers.

## Racing sulkies

French Trotters are generally raced in harness. The light, two-wheeled vehicles they pull are called sulkies. They are also raced under saddle. Some French Trotters are used for general riding and for breeding riding horses. They are good jumpers.

# Camargue

The Camargue region of the Rhône delta in France is a bleak and windy area. Here, the wild Camargue horses have lived on poor grazing for thousands of years. Some are tamed and ridden by local cowboys to round up wild black bulls.

## Wild white horses

Camargue ponies have been called the 'wild white horses of the sea'. They are small at 14hh (142cm), very tough and always white or grey in colour. They look like the horses in ancient cave paintings.

# Przewalski's Horse

I n the late 1870s, a Russian explorer named Nicolai Przewalski discovered a herd of pony-sized wild horses in the mountains of Mongolia, on the edge of the Gobi Desert. They looked similar to the primitive herds that once roamed Asia, and became known as Przewalski's Horse. Also called the Mongolian or Asiatic Wild Horse, Przewalski's Horse and the Tarpan are two surviving strains of four types of primitive horses which existed 10,000 years ago.

**The breed saved**
Przewalski's Horse is now extinct in the wild, but it is preserved in zoos and private studs.

## Stone Age horse

Between 16,000 and 27,000 years ago, early humans painted animals on the walls of caves. Some of the pictures were of horses that looked like the animal we call Przewalski's Horse. Amazingly, this breed has hardly changed at all over this long period of time.

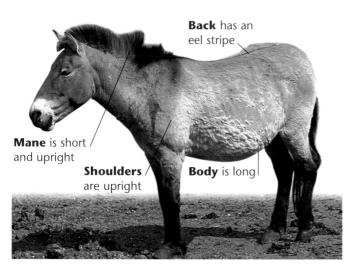

**Back** has an eel stripe

**Mane** is short and upright

**Shoulders** are upright

**Body** is long

## Facts and figures

| Przewalski's Horse | Tarpan |
| --- | --- |
| • **Height** 12–14.2hh (122–147cm) | • **Height** Around 13hh (132cm) |
| • **Colour** Yellow dun, with black points | • **Colour** Mouse dun, brown |

Przewalski's Horse has similar features to primitive horses. The body is dun with black points, and the legs may have zebra stripes. On the back is a black line called an eel stripe. The mane grows upright and there is little or no forelock. The muzzle and the areas around the eyes are pale in colour.

**Face to face**
Przewalski's Horses have large, plain heads with a convex or straight profile. Their eyes are set high up, so their heads look long.

# Tarpan

The Tarpan originally lived in Russia and in central and eastern Europe. The breed was domesticated, but in the 19th century, it became extinct. In the 1930s, a Polish professor named Vetulani found ponies living in Polish forests that were like the ancient breed. With careful breeding, he recreated the Tarpan.

**Quarters** slope steeply

**Neck** is short and thick

**Head** is large and Roman-nosed

**Body** is deep

**Legs** have zebra stripes

## Modern Tarpan

The new breed of Tarpan lives a natural life in herds on reserves owned by the Polish government. Despite its ancient ancestry, it is much less primitive-looking than Przewalski's Horse. Although its head is quite big and its neck is quite short, the Tarpan looks much more like a modern riding pony.

Although the original Tarpan is extinct, Professor Vetulani's new breed is so similar to the old one that some people consider it still exists. Like Przewalski's Horse, it has a dorsal stripe and zebra stripes on the legs. The Tarpan's mane and tail are long.

# Irish Draught

The Irish Draught was bred in its native Ireland as an all-round horse used for riding, driving and farm work. This breed dates back to the 12th century, and its ancestors include European heavy breeds and the Spanish Horse. It is large and strong, and capable of carrying a lot of weight.

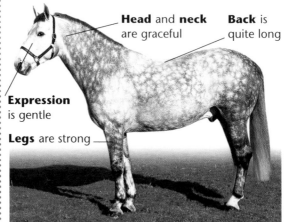

**Head** and **neck** are graceful

**Back** is quite long

**Expression** is gentle

**Legs** are strong

## Natural jumper

This breed is a natural jumper. Both the pure-bred Irish Draught and the Thoroughbred cross are often used for hunting. They can clear all kinds of obstacles when ridden on cross-country courses.

Despite its size – 16 to 17hh (163–173cm) – the Irish Draught is economical to keep. It has a calm temperament, and is easy to ride and handle. It can be any solid colour, but is often grey. Although it is not very fast, this big horse is athletic and agile.

# Hackney Horse

The Hackney Horse is an English breed that developed from two earlier breeds called the Norfolk Trotter and the Yorkshire Roadster. These were heavier, working horses, but the modern Hackney is more graceful because it was cross-bred with Thoroughbreds. The Hackney is now a show harness horse that delights spectators with its brilliant action and appearance.

This lightly built and compact horse gives the impression of having great energy. It is high-spirited and moves very freely, throwing its forelegs well forwards with each stride. The action must be straight when seen from the front or the back.

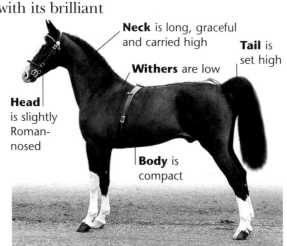

**Neck** is long, graceful and carried high

**Tail** is set high

**Withers** are low

**Head** is slightly Roman-nosed

**Body** is compact

## High-stepping horse

The Hackney's action, especially when trotting, is spectacular. It raises its knees and hocks very high, and as it moves, pauses slightly at each stride, giving the impression of an effortless, floating movement.

# Cleveland Bay

This is the oldest of the native British breeds. It has been bred in the north of England since the Middle Ages. Apart from Barb and Spanish crosses in the 17th century, the breed has been kept pure. These horses are strong, hardy, long-lived and good-natured.

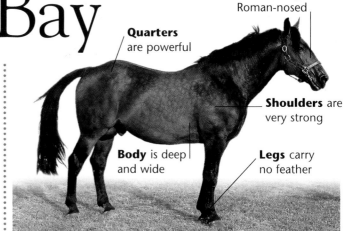

**Head** is large and Roman-nosed

**Quarters** are powerful

**Shoulders** are very strong

**Body** is deep and wide

**Legs** carry no feather

The Cleveland Bay is now classed as a rare breed. It is not used as a carriage horse so much nowadays, and is mainly used to cross with other breeds. As a result, the pure-bred Cleveland has almost disappeared.

## Royal team

The Royal Mews at Buckingham Palace in London, England, has Cleveland Bays, which pull the royal carriages. The Duke of Edinburgh (left) is driving a four-in-hand team, which competes in cross-country driving events.

## Key facts

- **Place of origin**
  North Yorkshire, England

- **Height**
  About 16.2hh (168cm)

- **Colour**
  Always bay with no white except a star

- **Uses**
  Driving, sometimes riding

# Andalucian

The Andalucian horse, from southern Spain, is the modern equivalent of the ancient Spanish Horse, which influenced horse breeding worldwide. Most American breeds are descended from the Spanish Horse. The Andalucian is noble and proud, agile and athletic, with a good temperament.

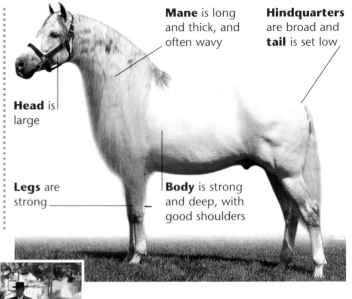

**Head** is large

**Mane** is long and thick, and often wavy

**Hindquarters** are broad and **tail** is set low

**Legs** are strong

**Body** is strong and deep, with good shoulders

## Ride and drive

Although it is mainly used for riding, and is a popular dressage horse, the Andalucian is also driven. In its native Spain, it is often used in harness during ceremonial and festive occasions.

The beautiful Andalucian horse stands between 15 and 16hh (152–163cm). It is bay or grey in colour, the grey sometimes having a pinkish tone. The Andalucian carries itself proudly, is athletic, although not fast, and has a kind and friendly nature.

# Lusitano

The Lusitano is similar to the Andalucian breed and is also descended from the Spanish Horse. It comes from Portugal, and was used by the Portuguese cavalry and for light farm work. This horse has spectacular high action, and it is taught 'high school' movements. It is also used as a carriage horse.

**Mane** and **tail** are full, long and often wavy

**Hindquarters** are sloping and **hindlegs** are long

**Profile** is straight or Roman-nosed

**Cannon bones** are long

**Back** is short, and ribs are well rounded

## Spanish walk

This horse is performing a special 'high school' movement called the Spanish walk, which it has been trained to do. In this gait, the forelegs are lifted up high and stretched out in front of the horse.

The Lusitano stands between 15 and 16hh (152–163cm), and it can be any solid colour. Grey is the most common colour, but this horse may also be bay, dun, chestnut or black. The Lusitano has a short, arched neck, sloping quarters and a compact body.

# Lipizzaner

The Lipizzaner is the horse used by the famous Spanish Riding School of Vienna, in Austria. It is descended from the ancient Spanish breed, which is how the school got its name. The word 'Lipizzaner' comes from Lipica, in Slovenia, where these horses were originally bred.

**From black to grey**
Lipizzaner foals are born black, and their coats gradually get lighter in colour as they grow older. They may be seven years or even older before they turn grey.

## Stocky horse

The Lipizzaner is stockily built, with short, strong legs. The shape of this horse's shoulders makes it suitable for use in harness as well as for riding. Its action tends to be high, and its feet are strong. It is an extremely intelligent horse.

## Spanish school

The Spanish Riding School trains Lipizzaner stallions to perform high school movements in an 18th-century arena lit by large chandeliers. It takes many years to train both the horses and their riders.

### Key facts

- **Place of origin**
  Lipica, Slovenia

- **Height**
  15.1–16.2hh
  (155–168cm)

- **Colour**
  Usually grey, but sometimes bay

- **Uses**
  General riding, and as a carriage horse

- **Characteristics**
  Intelligent, docile and long-lived

**Levade**
The 'levade' is a classical high school movement. The horse rears up and balances on its hind legs.

**Head** is often Roman-nosed

**Hindquarters** are powerful

**Body** is long and **withers** low

**Neck** is short and thick

**Legs** are powerful

# Morgan

**Profile** may be concave, giving an Arab look

**Neck** is arched

**Quarters** are muscular and well-rounded

**Legs** are strong and joints flat

**Shoulders** slope

The Morgan comes from the eastern states of Massachusetts and Vermont in the USA. Morgans are descended from a stallion born in 1789, named Justin Morgan, after his owner. This horse worked on the farm, and raced, both in harness and under saddle.

## Specially shod

Morgans are shown in either Park or Pleasure classes. Horses shown in the Park classes have their feet trimmed and shod to produce a high action. If this is not done, the action is normal.

Standing between 14.2 and 15.2hh (147–157cm), the Morgan is bay, brown, chestnut or black in colour. It is spirited, intelligent and alert, but has a good temperament, and is easy to handle. Hardy, strong and full of stamina, it is both ridden and driven.

# Criollo

Descended from Spanish horses brought to South America in the 16th century, the Criollo is considered to be the toughest and soundest breed of horse in the world. The breed is native to the grassy plains of Argentina, where it is used by the gauchos, or cowboys, to work cattle. The Criollo is also found in Brazil, Uruguay, Chile, Peru and Venezuela.

The Criollo can survive on little food in harsh climates. It is long-lived, and has great stamina. In the 1920s, Professor Aimé Tschiffely rode two Criollo ponies, called Mancha and Gato, from Buenos Aires in South America to New York in the USA. The total distance was 16,000km.

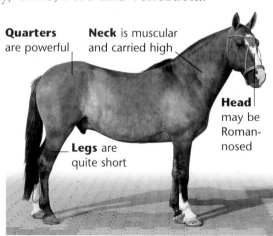

**Quarters** are powerful

**Neck** is muscular and carried high

**Head** may be Roman-nosed

**Legs** are quite short

## Polo pony

Criollos are 14 to 15hh (142–152cm) and are usually dun in colour, with dark points and an eel stripe. They are often crossed with Thoroughbreds to produce the famous Argentinian polo ponies.

# Quarter Horse

This first 'all-American' horse was bred in Virginia in the 17th century for riding and farm work. Its speed and agility made it perfect for working cattle. The breed is so-named because English settlers used to race these horses over quarter-mile (402m) tracks.

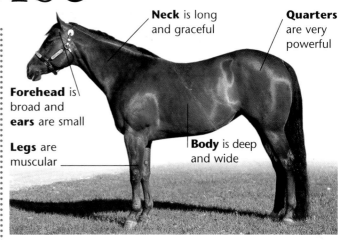

Neck is long and graceful

Quarters are very powerful

Forehead is broad and ears are small

Legs are muscular

Body is deep and wide

## Facts and figures

- **Place of origin**
  Virginia, USA

- **Height**
  15–16hh (152–163cm)

- **Colour**
  Any solid colour

- **Uses**
  Working cattle, showing

It has been claimed that the Quarter Horse is the most popular horse in the world, with over three million registered in the USA. Agile and athletic, yet with a calm temperament, it is an ideal riding horse, as well as being superb at working cattle and performing at Western horse shows.

## Sliding halt

A horse that works with cattle must be able to start, stop and turn very quickly. In Western horse shows, one of the most dramatic movements is the sliding halt, where the horse stops instantly (right). Special shoes on the hind feet allow them to slide.

# Pinto

The Pinto is a colour type rather than a breed, though there are two Pinto breed societies in the United States. Descended from 16th-century Spanish horses, it has become popular in the United States. Pintos can be black and white (piebald), or chestnut or brown and white (skewbald).

'Pinto' comes from the Spanish word *pintado*, which means 'painted'. There are two main colour types: overo, which is mostly coloured with white patches, and tobiano, which is mostly white with coloured patches (rearing horse, far right). Pintos may vary in size and shape.

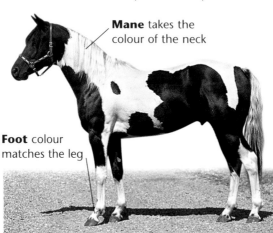

**Mane** takes the colour of the neck

**Foot** colour matches the leg

## Native favourites

Pintos were favourites of the Native Americans because their colouring provided good camouflage. Today, they are often bred for their colour rather than their shape, and points are awarded for their markings.

# Palomino

This is another colour type rather than a breed, so Palominos may be any size. The coat colour should be as near as possible to that of a new gold coin, with a white mane and tail. Palominos were brought to the USA by the Spanish in the 15th and 16th centuries.

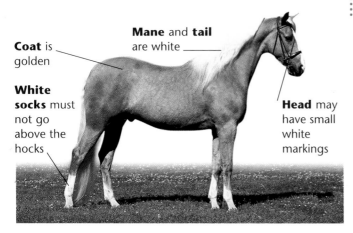

**Coat** is golden

**Mane** and **tail** are white

**White socks** must not go above the hocks

**Head** may have small white markings

Palominos are bred by crossing palomino-coloured horses with chestnuts, or chestnuts with creams or albinos. In 15th-century Spain, the palomino colour was a favourite of the powerful Queen Isabella.

## Barrel racing

Palominos may be of any size or type and can be used for many activities, including showing and Western classes, as well as for general riding. This horse is negotiating a tight turn at a gallop as part of a barrel race in Tampa, Florida.

# Appaloosa

This breed gets its name from the Palouse River in Washington State, USA. It was bred as a workhorse by the Nez Percé tribe of native Americans in the 18th century, from imported Spanish horses. Quarter Horses have been used to improve the breed, making it a strong, compact and good-natured horse. It is agile and athletic, has great stamina and is a good jumper.

**Eye** has a white ring

**Mane** and **tail** are sparse

**White** over quarters is blanket marking

**Shoulders** are sloping

**Feet** may have vertical stripes

The main markings are leopard (white coat with dark spots – below); frost (dark background with white speckles); blanket (white quarters and loins, sometimes with dark spots); marble (roan, with a frost pattern in the centre of the body and darker round the edges); and snowflake (dark background with white spots).

## Facts and figures

- **Place of origin**
  Washington State, USA

- **Height**
  14.2–15.2hh (147–157cm)

- **Colour**
  White with dark markings

- **Uses**
  Riding, showing, jumping

# Tennessee Walking Horse

This breed was developed in the 18th and 19th centuries by plantation, or estate, owners of the southern United States, who wanted a comfortable riding horse to carry them round their large areas of land. It is called a 'gaited horse', because it can perform three extra gaits – the flat walk, the running walk and the rocking-chair canter. All these movements are smooth and comfortable for the rider.

The Tennessee Walking Horse is a popular riding horse for all members of the family in the USA, as well as a show horse. The breed stands 15 to 16hh (152–163cm) and is usually brown, bay, chestnut or black. It is said to be the most good-tempered of all horses.

**Mane** is clipped off at the top in the USA

**Head** is large

**Shoulders** are muscular

**Legs** are strong

**Back** is short

**Tail** is set high

# American Saddlebred

The Saddlebred was bred in Kentucky, USA, in the 19th century. It is another 'gaited' horse: three-gaited horses perform the walk, trot and canter with high steps; five-gaited horses also perform the slow gait and the rack, both four-beat, lateral paces. The way the horse is shod accentuates its action.

The Saddlebred is usually bay, brown or chestnut, and stands 15 to 16hh (152–163cm). Nicking the dock muscles makes it carry its tail higher. It is mostly a show horse, but if it is shod normally, it can be used for harness or general riding.

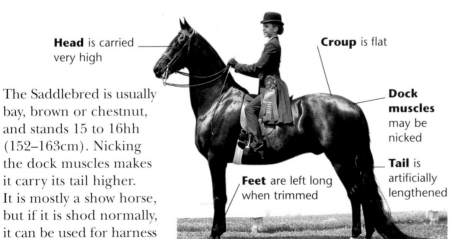

**Head** is carried very high

**Croup** is flat

**Dock muscles** may be nicked

**Tail** is artificially lengthened

**Feet** are left long when trimmed

## Spectacular action

The rack (above) is a fast and spectacular pace in which each leg is raised high and lands separately. Special boots protect the front heels and pasterns from being injured by the horse's hind feet as they reach far forwards.

# Missouri Foxtrotter

This horse was bred in the 19th century in Arkansas and Missouri in the USA as a comfortable riding horse that could cover long distances quite quickly. The breed has a unique gait called a 'foxtrot', in which it walks with its front legs and trots with its hind legs.

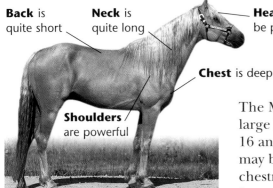

**Back** is quite short

**Neck** is quite long

**Head** may be plain

**Chest** is deep

**Shoulders** are powerful

The Missouri Foxtrotter is a large horse which stands between 16 and 17hh (163–173 cm). It may be any colour, but most are chestnut. This breed is sure-footed and has a gentle nature.

## Comfortable ride

The Foxtrotter's gait is smooth and comfortable. It can travel at a speed of 8km/h for long distances, and may go twice as fast over shorter distances. This breed is used for trail riding and showing.

# Standardbred

The Standardbred is the fastest harness racing horse in the world. It was first bred in the USA in the 19th century. Most Standardbreds are descended from an English Thoroughbred, which also had Norfolk Trotter ancestors. Standardbreds race either as trotters or pacers.

The Standardbred is about 15.2hh (157cm) and is usually bay, brown or chestnut. More heavily built than the Thoroughbred, it is fast and has great stamina. This horse can cover 1.6km in one minute 54 seconds.

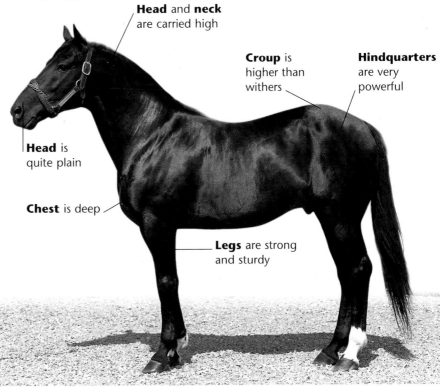

**Head** and **neck** are carried high

**Croup** is higher than withers

**Hindquarters** are very powerful

**Head** is quite plain

**Chest** is deep

**Legs** are strong and sturdy

# Mustang

The tough wild horses that once roamed the plains of the western USA are called Mustangs. They are descended from Spanish horses taken to America in the 16th century, which were turned loose or escaped and became wild. For centuries, Mustangs lived a natural life. Today, special efforts are made to protect the original type of wild horse.

Mustangs range in height from 13.2 to 15hh (137–152cm) and may be any colour. They are fast, strong, agile and hardy. They do not always have good natures, but some are domesticated and used as riding and endurance horses.

**Head** may be Roman-nosed

**Legs** are strong and tough

**Body** is compact

## In the wild

Mustangs were rounded up and used by cowboys for cattle herding. Some were tamed and ridden by Native Americans, and others were hunted. As a result, their numbers fell, but they are now protected by US law.

# Waler

The oddly named Waler is Australian – its name comes from 'New South Wales'. It was bred from Basuto ponies, Arabs, Barbs and Thoroughbreds to work on the huge Australian cattle and sheep ranches. It was a cavalry horse in the Boer War and the First World War. It is also now used for police work.

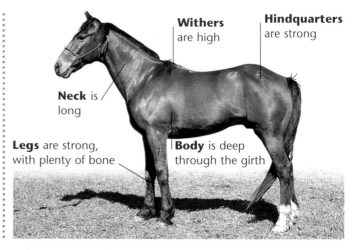

**Withers** are high

**Hindquarters** are strong

**Neck** is long

**Legs** are strong, with plenty of bone

**Body** is deep through the girth

## Riding horse

The Waler is sometimes called the Australian Stock Horse, but it is also an ideal horse for general riding. It is fast and agile and is a natural jumper. Some Walers perform at rodeos, doing displays of buckjumping.

The Waler ranges in height from 14.2 to 16hh (147–163cm) and may be any solid colour. It is more powerfully built than the Thoroughbred. It is strong and tough, and its great powers of endurance mean that it can be ridden round the ranch all day.

# Pony Breeds

**P**onies are smaller than horses and have different features. They are deeper through the girth and have shorter legs. They often have feather on the lower legs, and thick manes and tails. Ponies are sure-footed, and usually full of character.

# Dartmoor

**Head** is small and neat

**Shoulders** are sloping

**Legs** are strong

**Feet** are hard

**Body** is compact and well-formed

Small ponies have lived wild on Dartmoor in Devon, England, for hundreds of years. Poor grazing and harsh conditions on the moors have produced strong, tough animals. Over the centuries, Arab, Thoroughbred and Welsh Section A crosses have been used to improve the quality of this breed.

The Dartmoor is a first-class children's riding pony. It is strong enough to carry a heavy weight, has good paces, jumps well and has a good temperament. It stands around 12.2hh (127cm) and is bay or brown in colour.

## Wild on the moor

There are not many pure-bred ponies living wild on Dartmoor today. Most of them are bred in studs. The ponies roaming the moor look quite different. In winter, to withstand the wind, rain and snow of their native home, they grow very thick coats and long, shaggy manes and tails.

# Exmoor

This pony is from the region of southwest England known as Exmoor. It is one of the oldest breeds in the world, and dates back to the Ice Age. Today it is classed as a rare breed. It is only 12.2 to 12.3hh (127–130cm), but is strong enough to carry an adult.

**Eye** is hooded, with a light ring round it, called a 'toad' eye

**Muzzle** is light-coloured

**Back** is broad

**Tail** is wide at the top

**Legs** are short and strong

The Exmoor is usually a mousy dun colour, with light, mealy-coloured areas round the eye, muzzle, inside of the legs and underside of the belly. The ponies may also be bay or brown.

**Head** is small and neat

**Hindquarters** are strong and give speed and jumping ability

**Shoulders** are sloping

**Legs** are strong, with plenty of bone

**Body** is compact and deep through the girth

# Connemara

The Connemara comes from the moors of western Ireland, where its ancestors have lived since the 16th century. Native ponies were crossed with Spanish, Barb, Arab, Welsh Cob and Thoroughbred horses to develop the breed. The result is a strong, sturdy riding pony, with good paces and jumping ability.

Connemaras can be grey, dun, bay, brown, black, chestnut or roan. They are 13 to 14.2hh (132–147cm) and are hardy, docile and intelligent. They are ridden by both children and adults, and make good competition horses when crossed with Thoroughbreds.

# New Forest

Since the 11th century, ponies have lived in the New Forest in Hampshire, England. Over the years, different breeds have been introduced, as well as Arabs and Barbs, so New Forest ponies have a mixture of ancestors. They are fast and have good, low action.

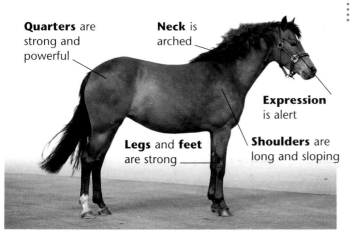

**Quarters** are strong and powerful

**Neck** is arched

**Expression** is alert

**Legs** and **feet** are strong

**Shoulders** are long and sloping

There are two types of pony – one stands up to 13.1hh (135cm), and the other 13.2 to 14.2hh (137–147cm). Both are narrow in build, making them easy for children to ride. The ponies may be of any solid colour.

## Forest pony

Most of the New Forest is heathland. Local people, known as Commoners, are allowed to keep ponies there. Many of these are in poor condition. The better examples of the breed usually come from stud farms.

# Welsh Section A

The Welsh Section A, or Welsh Mountain Pony, has lived on the hills of Wales in Britain since pre-Roman times. It is thought to be the most beautiful pony breed. Strong and tough, with great powers of endurance, it is used for riding and driving.

Section A ponies should not be taller than 12hh (122cm). They look like miniature Arabs, and are strong for their size. They may be any solid colour, are sure-footed and intelligent, and make good riding ponies.

**Head** is small and dished

**Neck** is long and graceful

**Back** is short and strong

**Body** is deep through the girth

**Legs** are sturdy

# Welsh Section B

The Welsh Section B is also called the Welsh Pony. It was bred by crossing Section As with Section Ds, and has Arab ancestors as well. Originally the pony was used by farmers for transport and for herding sheep grazing on the Welsh hills. The modern type of this breed has existed since the early 20th century.

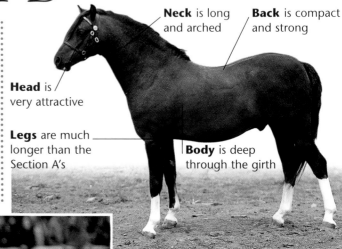

**Neck** is long and arched

**Back** is compact and strong

**Head** is very attractive

**Legs** are much longer than the Section A's

**Body** is deep through the girth

Section B ponies are 12.2 to 13.2hh (127–137cm) and may be any solid colour. They have the character and gentle nature of the Section A, but make more useful riding ponies because of their longer legs.

## Competitive pony

As the Section B is taller than the Welsh Mountain Pony, it can be ridden by larger children and used in competitions such as gymkhana events. It has long, low action, and is also a good jumper.

# Welsh Section C

This pony was originally bred by crossing the Section A and Section D, and is known as the Welsh Pony of Cob Type. Smaller than the Welsh Cob, but stockier in build than the Welsh Pony, it was once used for all kinds of farm work, as well as in the slate quarries of North Wales. Today it is often used for trekking and trail riding, as well as driving.

**Neck** is thick and carried high

**Quarters** are very muscular

**Head** is attractive

**Shoulders** are powerful

**Legs** are strong

This small pony should not be taller than 13.2hh (137cm). Despite its size, the Section C is very strong. It is also hardy enough to live outside all year round. It has a good temperament and may be any solid colour.

## Driving pony

With their fast action, Section C ponies are ideal for driving. They are also good riding ponies, can jump well, and are strong enough to carry light adults as well as children.

# Welsh Section D

The Section D, or Welsh Cob, was bred from the Welsh Mountain Pony, with crosses to Spanish horses, trotters and Arabs between the 11th and 19th centuries. The Cob was used for all-round farm work and riding, and for pulling carts in cities.

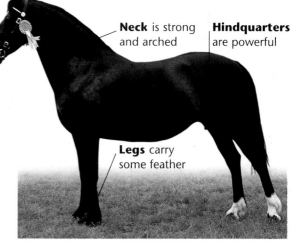

**Head** looks like a pony's

**Neck** is strong and arched

**Hindquarters** are powerful

**Legs** carry some feather

The Section D stands between 14.2 and 15.2hh (147–157cm) and may be any solid colour. It is famous for its fast, high-stepping trot, is an ideal driving pony, a good jumper, and is also used for riding and trekking.

# Fell

This breed of pony is about 2,000 years old. Fell ponies come from Cumbria, England, and have Friesian ancestors. They were used as pack animals to carry lead from the mines to the docks, and often travelled 386km in a week. They were also ridden and driven, and used for farm work and herding.

These ponies are only 14hh (142cm), but they can carry 100kg packs or be ridden by adult riders. They are strong, hardy, sure-footed and energetic. They are always black or dark brown, with only small white markings allowed.

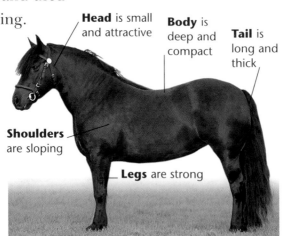

**Head** is small and attractive

**Body** is deep and compact

**Tail** is long and thick

**Shoulders** are sloping

**Legs** are strong

## Good riding pony

The Fell's sloping shoulders make it more suitable for riding than the Dales pony, and it can be ridden by everyone in the family. It is also used for trekking. The Fell does well in harness and is popular for competition driving.

# Dales

This strong and sturdy pony comes from Durham, North Yorkshire and Northumberland, England. It was also used as a pack pony to carry lead across the hills. The breed is about 2,000 years old, and has Welsh Cob and Clydesdale ancestors.

The Dales is more of a harness pony than the Fell. It is taller, more solidly built and has higher knee action. It is about 14.2hh (147cm) and is usually black in colour. The Dales is also used for general riding.

**Neck** is thick and arched

**Back** is strong and muscular

**Head** looks like a pony's

**Chest** is broad and deep

**Legs** are short and strong and carry feather

# Highland

The Highland has existed in Scotland since the last Ice Age and is the largest of Britain's pony breeds. They were bred for farm work, forestry and deer-stalking, and there were three sizes – the smallest from the islands and the largest from the mainland. Today, there is little difference between the three.

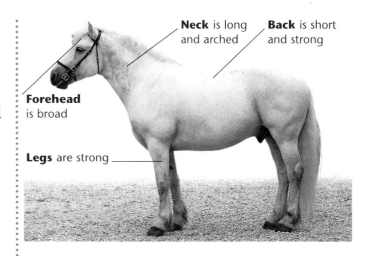

**Neck** is long and arched

**Back** is short and strong

**Forehead** is broad

**Legs** are strong

Powerfully built and very strong, the Highland looks like some of the ponies that are seen in ancient cave paintings. It often has an eel stripe along its back and zebra markings on its legs. Its shoulders are massive and its feet are hard and tough. It is long-lived, easy to keep and has a docile, gentle nature.

## Facts and figures

- **Place of origin**
  Scottish Highlands, UK

- **Height**
  13–14.2hh (132–147cm)

- **Colour**
  Grey, dun, brown, black

- **Uses**
  Riding, trekking, harness

**Champion pony**
The champion Highland stallion Duart of Glenmuick (right) has the breed's characteristic full mane and tail.

# Fjord

The Fjord is an ancient breed descended from Przewalski's Horse. It has many characteristics of primitive horses, being dun in colour, with a dorsal stripe and sometimes zebra stripes on its legs. The Fjord is strong and sure-footed, hardy and economical to keep, and has great powers of endurance.

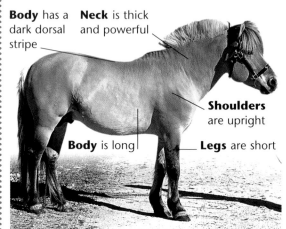

**Body** has a dark dorsal stripe

**Neck** is thick and powerful

**Shoulders** are upright

**Body** is long

**Legs** are short

## Special mane

The Fjord's mane is dark in the centre and silvery white on the outside. It is cut to stand upright, in a long curve, with the outer hair shorter than at the centre.

The Vikings used ponies that looked like the Fjord, and shipped them in longboats to Scotland and Iceland. Since ancient times, this pony has been used for work on mountain farms, as well as being a riding and pack pony. The pony stands between 13 and 14.2hh (132–147cm).

# Icelandic

Although the Icelandic is only small, people call it a horse. It stands between 12.3 and 13.2hh (130–137cm), but is strong enough to carry an adult for long distances. The Vikings brought these ponies to Iceland, and the breed has been kept pure for 1,000 years. Icelandics are ridden, driven and used for trekking.

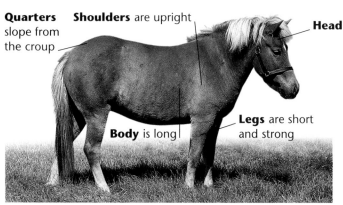

**Quarters** slope from the croup

**Shoulders** are upright

**Head** is large

**Body** is long

**Legs** are short and strong

As well as walking, trotting, cantering and galloping, Icelandic ponies can perform a gait called the *skeid*, which is pacing, and the *tölt*, which is a fast, running walk. They take part in competitions for gaited horses.

## Outdoor pony

Although the Icelandic winter is harsh, these ponies often live outside in a semi-wild state. This makes them tough and hardy. They are also very sure-footed, moving easily over the rough and mountainous ground of their island home.

# Haflinger

These ponies have been bred in the Austrian mountains for over 200 years. All native Haflingers have a brand mark – a letter 'H' and an edelweiss, the national flower of Austria. They were used for all kinds of farm and forestry work, as well as for riding. They are now popular trekking ponies.

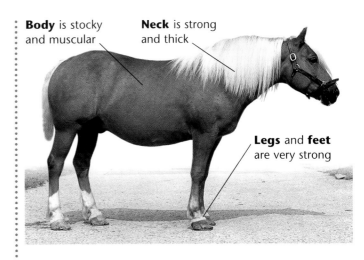

**Body** is stocky and muscular

**Neck** is strong and thick

**Legs** and **feet** are very strong

As well as being sturdy and tough, Haflingers usually live for a long time. They start working at four years old, and may continue until the age of 40 – almost twice as long as the average horse. Haflingers have a docile temperament and are easy to handle.

## Facts and figures

- **Place of origin**
  Austrian Tyrol, Europe

- **Height**
  13.1–14.2hh (135–147cm)

- **Colour**
  Chestnut or palomino

- **Uses**
  Riding, trekking, harness

**Sleigh ride**
Haflingers pull sleighs in winter. Their harness may be decorated for Christmas.

# New breeds of the USA

Some stallions produce foals that have similar characteristics to their sire, or father. This quality is called 'prepotency', and horses that have it may be used to start new breeds. Once a breed is established, a stud book is set up in which horses that meet the breed's standards are registered.

**Body** is well-proportioned

**Neck** is long, arched and graceful

**Head** shows pony's Spanish ancestry

**Feet** are strong

## Rocky Mountain

This pony may be the world's most recent breed, as the stud book registrations only began in 1986. Although there are other colours, the favourite is a unique chocolate brown with a flaxen mane and tail. The Rocky Mountain is sometimes called a horse because of its height. It is hardy, and can survive in harsh winter weather.

**Ears** are exceptionally long

**Show driving**
The American Shetland, driven to a show carriage, is a popular attraction in the USA. This pony also races in harness, and some types are ridden and jumped in the show ring.

## American Shetland

This pony is very different from the Shetland of the British Isles. The breed was developed in the 1880s by crossing lightly built Shetlands with Hackney Ponies, and the result is a Hackney-type show harness pony.

**Head** is more like a horse's than a pony's

**Head and neck carriage** are like those of the Hackney Pony

**Mane** and **tail** are long and thick

**Body** is long and narrow

**Ponies** often stand with legs stretched out

**Special gait**
Although this graceful pony is cantering, the characteristic action of the Rocky Mountain is pacing. In this gait, both legs on the same side move together. The Rocky Mountain can reach speeds of up to 25km/h when pacing.

## Facts and figures

**Rocky Mountain Pony**
- **Height**
  14.2–15hh (147–152cm)

- **Colour**
  Chocolate, with flaxen mane and tail, plus others

**American Shetland**
- **Height**
  Up to 11.2hh (117cm)

- **Colour**
  Any solid colour

**Pony of the Americas**
- **Height**
  11.2–13hh (117–132cm)

- **Colour**
  Markings are the same as the Appaloosa

# Pony of the Americas

This breed was started in Iowa in the 1950s when a Shetland pony was crossed with an Appaloosa. The foal that they produced was the first of the breed. Ponies of the Americas are small and stocky, and have the traditional Appaloosa markings. These ponies are docile and good-natured.

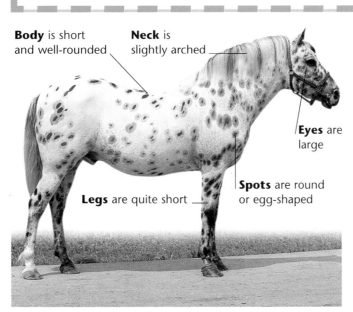

**Body** is short and well-rounded

**Neck** is slightly arched

**Eyes** are large

**Spots** are round or egg-shaped

**Legs** are quite short

**On the leading rein**
These ponies are small and easy to handle, so they are good for children who are learning to ride. First lessons are often on a leading rein.

# Caspian

The Caspian is possibly the oldest breed of horse or pony that exists, and it may be the ancestor of the Arab. Since prehistoric times it has lived near the southern coast of the Caspian Sea, in what is now Iran. In the mid-20th century, the breed was rediscovered, and these ponies are now bred in Europe, America, Australia and New Zealand.

The Caspian looks more like a miniature horse than a pony. It is lightly built, has a fine, silky coat, mane and tail, and is very fast for its size. The Caspian stands 10 to 12hh (102–122cm), and it is usually bay or chestnut in colour.

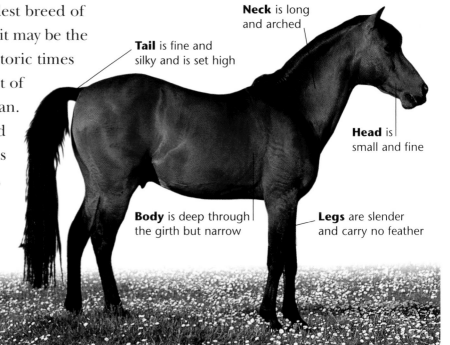

**Neck** is long and arched

**Tail** is fine and silky and is set high

**Head** is small and fine

**Body** is deep through the girth but narrow

**Legs** are slender and carry no feather

# Chincoteague and Assateague

Chincoteague and Assateague are islands off the coast of Virginia, USA, where these small wild ponies have lived since the 16th century. They may be the descendants of Barb horses that were once shipwrecked there.

**Quarters** slope sharply from the croup

**Back** is short

**Head** may be large and plain

These ponies have lived on islands for hundreds of years so they have not been crossed with other breeds. They are about 12hh (122cm) and may be any colour. They are often skewbald or piebald (see Pinto page 42).

## Island ponies

Once a year, the Assateague ponies are taken across to Chincoteague island, where the young animals are sold. These ponies are strong-willed and can be difficult to handle, but some are used for riding.

# Basuto

This pony is named after the area of South Africa where it was developed between the 17th and 19th centuries. It has Arab, Barb and Thoroughbred ancestors. The Basuto often had to endure harsh conditions, so this breed is strong and tough. The British used Basuto ponies during the Boer War.

**Head** may have Arab features

**Neck** is thin

**Back** is long

**Shoulders** are upright

**Feet** are hard

The Basuto is about 14.2hh (147cm). It has great stamina, and can be ridden every day for many miles. This makes the Basuto a popular trekking pony. It is usually brown, bay, grey or chestnut in colour.

## Herding pony

Farmers in Lesotho, Africa, use Basuto ponies for herding animals, as well as for riding round their land. In the past, these ponies have been raced, and also used by the army and for polo. They are popular general riding ponies in southern Africa.

# Boer

**Neck** is long and carried high

The Boer pony developed in the 19th century in South Africa, and has similar ancestors to the Basuto. Most Boer ponies did not have to endure such harsh conditions as the Basuto, so this breed is often taller and of better quality. The Boer is known as the 'Boerperd' in its native country. It is found in the north-eastern part of South Africa, where it is used as an all-round farm horse.

**Expression** is alert

**Pasterns** are long and sloping

**Body** is narrow

**Legs** are long and slender

The Boer's height ranges from 13.3 to 15.3hh (140–160cm) and it may be any solid colour, including palomino. Some Boers are five-gaited, and can perform the slow gait and rack as well as the walk, trot and canter. They are popular endurance horses.

# Australian

**P**onies were first brought to Australia in the early 19th century, and in the 20th century, the Australian pony officially became a breed. Its ancestors include the Hackney, the Shetland, the Arab, the Thoroughbred and the Welsh Mountain Pony (Section A), which it closely resembles.

The Australian pony stands between 12 and 14hh (122–142cm) and is an attractive animal. Its action is free and level, and it is good-natured and easy to handle. This breed may be any solid colour and in Australia it is a popular riding and show pony.

**Neck** is arched and elegant

**Quarters** are well developed

**Head** is small, neat and attractive

**Body** is compact and strong

**Shoulders** are sloping

## Tiny foal

Falabella foals are only about 4hh (41cm), but they grow quickly. When the mother is pregnant, she carries her foal for 13 months, which is two months longer than other horses and ponies.

# Falabella

**T**he little Falabella is named after the family who created it near Buenos Aires, Argentina, in the early 20th century. They crossed tiny Shetland ponies with a small Thoroughbred, and kept breeding from the smallest ponies produced. Falabellas are 'inbred' so they are not strong, and need looking after carefully. They are not ridden, though they are sometimes driven. Falabellas are mostly kept as pets.

**Mane** and **tail** are thick

**Tail** is set low

**Legs** are not very strong

**Body** is deep

**Head** is large

Falabellas are about 7 to 8.2hh (71–86cm) and may be any colour. People think of them as miniature horses rather than small ponies, as they have fine bones and slender legs. They are clever and friendly, and make good pets.

# Shetland

The Shetland is the smallest of Britain's mountain and moorland ponies. It has lived in the bleak Shetland Islands, north-east of Scotland, for about 10,000 years. The harsh climate and poor grazing have made it very hardy. For its size, the Shetland is probably the strongest of all horses and ponies.

**Body** is deep and compact

**Tail** is full

**Head** is neat

**Legs** are short

Shetlands are measured in inches, not in hands, and are up to 42in (107cm) high. They can be any colour. They are used as children's riding ponies, and in harness, where they are especially good at scurry driving.

## Tough ponies

These ponies can survive in the snow and strong winds of their island home. They grow thick coats and can live on very little food. Their small size means they can find shelter more easily than larger ponies.

# Hackney

The Hackney Pony is a smaller, pony-like version of the Hackney Horse. The breed was produced in the 19th century from Fell and Welsh ponies and the Yorkshire Trotter. These early ponies were very hardy, and today's Hackneys are strong and tough, with great stamina. Hackneys have a high neck carriage, short, compact bodies and long, powerful legs. They can be 12.2 to 14hh (127–142cm), and are brown, bay or black.

## Spectacular action

The Hackney's high-stepping action is a spectacular sight, and produces much applause in the show ring. About 100 years ago, these ponies could be seen on city streets, where they were used by tradesmen delivering goods. Today, they are almost always show harness ponies.

# Glossary

You may not understand all the words you come across as you read about horses and ponies, and get to know more about their world. This list explains what some of the words mean.

*Appaloosa*

*Oldenburg*

**acquired mark**  A mark on a horse's or pony's body that is the result of an injury.

**action**  The way that a horse or pony moves. 'High action' means that the legs are lifted high off the ground and 'low action' means that they are kept close to the ground.

**blaze**  A white mark down the front of a horse's face.

**bone**  The measurement round the **cannon bone**, just below the knee. '**Plenty of bone**' means a high measurement and therefore strong legs.

**brand mark**  A mark that is burned into a horse's skin with a hot iron. Brand marks show that an animal belongs to a certain breed or person.

**breed society**  An organization that regulates the breeding of its particular breed of horse or pony.

**buckjumping**  Leaping in the air with all four feet at once and the back arched.

**cannon bone**  The bone in the foreleg between the **knee** and the **fetlock**.

**clean-legged**  Legs that carry no **feather**.

**coat**  The hair covering an animal's skin.

**cob**  A short-legged, stocky riding horse.

**competition horse**  A horse that takes part in competitions, usually eventing, dressage or showjumping.

**conformation**  The overall shape and proportions of a horse or pony.

**crest**  The centre of the arch on the **top line** of the neck.

**cross-country**  A riding course with jumps which must be completed within a specified time. Cross-country is part of **eventing.**

**croup**  The highest point of the hindquarters.

**deep through the girth**  Deep and broad through the chest and behind the **elbows**. This gives lots of space for the heart and lungs.

**diagonal**  When a horse trots, its legs move in diagonal pairs. This means that the right **hind leg** and left **foreleg** move at the same time.

**dished face**  A face that is concave, or curving inwards, in profile, like the Arab's.

**docile**  Quiet and calm.

**dock**  The top of a horse's tail.

**dorsal stripe**  A line that runs along the back – see **eel stripe**.

**draught horse**  A big, heavy horse used for pulling loads or farm implements.

**dressage**  The advanced schooling and training of a horse, performed in competitions.

**driving**  Today, driving is an equestrian sport and there are different types of competition.

**eel stripe**  A dark stripe along a horse's or pony's back, from its mane to its tail.

**elbow**  The joint at the top of the **foreleg**.

**endurance riding**  A long-distance riding competition.

**eventing**  A competition made up of **dressage**, **cross-country** and **showjumping**.

**feather**  The long hair that grows on the lower part of the legs of most heavy horses and some ponies.

**fetlock**  The joint on the lower part of a horse's leg, just above the foot.

**forearm**  The upper part of the **foreleg**.

**foreleg**  The front leg.

**forelock**  The part of a horse's or pony's mane that falls over the forehead.

**four-beat pace**  One in which each foot hits the ground separately, such as the walk.

**four-in-hand**  A team of four driving horses, with two in front and two behind.

**gait**  The **pace** at which a horse or pony moves. The four natural gaits are walk, trot, canter and gallop.

**gaited**  An American term describing a horse that can perform more gaits than the natural ones. Horses may be three-gaited or five-gaited.

**girth**  a) The part of a horse where the saddle's girth fits, just behind the forelegs. b) The broad strap that holds the saddle in place.

**gymkhana**  Games and races on horseback; an event usually held as part of a show.

**hack**  A riding horse.

**hand**  A horse's or pony's height is measured in hands. One hand equals 10cm.

**harness**  The equipment used on a horse that is being driven. '**In harness**' means being driven.

**hh**  Stands for 'hands high'.

**hind leg**  The back leg.

**hindquarters**  The rump.

**hock**  The joint halfway down the **hind leg**.

**hogging**  Cutting off a horse's or pony's mane.

*Shire*

*Welsh ponies*

*Solid colour*

*Part-coloured*

*Thoroughbreds*

**hunter** A horse used for hunting. It must be able to gallop and jump well.

**inbred** Bred from animals that are closely related to each other.

**in hand** Leading a horse or pony while on foot.

**in harness** *see* **harness**.

**knee** The joint halfway down the **foreleg**.

**lateral** At the side. A lateral **pace** is when both legs on the same side move together.

**living out** Living in a field rather than a stable.

**markings, record of** A horse's or pony's markings are recorded on vaccination certificates and passports.

**mealy** Light-coloured, the colour of oatmeal.

**nicking (of dock muscles)** In some American horses, the dock muscles are cut and reset to make the horse carry its tail higher.

**Norfolk Trotter** A fast-trotting harness horse that existed between the 15th and mid-20th centuries; ancestor of the Hackney and others.

**pace** a) Another word for **gait**. b) A gait in which both legs on the same side of a horse move together.

**pack pony** A pony that carries heavy loads in packs that are strapped to its back.

**part-bred** A horse or pony that has one **pure-bred**

parent, or two pure-bred parents of different breeds.

**part-coloured** When a horse is more than one colour, such as skewbald.

**pastern** The part of the horse's leg between the **fetlock** and the foot.

**pedigree** A table that lists an animal's parents, grandparents, great-grandparents etc.

**plain head** An unattractive or ugly head.

**point of the shoulder** The front of the shoulder joint, where the shoulder blade joins the first bone of the animal's **foreleg**.

**points** a) The physical features of a horse. b) The parts of a bay or dun horse that are black (the mane, tail and lower legs).

**pony-like head** A small, neat head with small ears and large eyes.

**presence** The way that a horse or pony carries itself.

**primitive** When it is used to describe a breed, 'primitive' means at an early stage of evolution.

**pure-bred** A horse or pony that has two parents of the same breed **registered** in the breed's **stud book**.

**quarters** Another word for **hindquarters**.

**rack** A fast **pace** in which each foot hits the ground separately.

**registered** Listed in the **stud book** of the breed to which the horse or pony belongs.

**Roman nose** A nose that, seen in profile, is convex, or curving outwards.

**scurry driving** A speed driving competition which uses small ponies in pairs.

**showing** Exhibiting a horse or pony at a horse show, where it is judged on its **conformation** and **paces**.

**showjumping** A jumping competition at a horse show.

**sloping shoulders** Shoulders that slope from the **withers** to the **point of the shoulder**. They give smooth, comfortable **paces** in a riding horse.

**slow gait** A slow, **four-beat**, high-stepping **gait**.

**solid colour** The same colour all over, with markings only on the legs and face.

**sound** A 'sound' horse is a healthy one, with no lameness or breathing problems.

**Spanish Horse** The most important European breed of horse for centuries, which had a huge impact on horse breeding throughout the world. Most American breeds are descended from the Spanish Horse.

**stamina** The ability to keep going even when very tired.

**straight action** Moving the legs straight forwards and backwards without any sideways movement.

**straight shoulders** *see* **upright shoulders**.

**stud book** A book in which the name, date of birth and **pedigree** of a **pure-bred** horse or pony is **registered**, or listed. Every horse and pony breed has a stud book.

**stud farm** A place where horses or ponies are bred. These are also referred to as 'studs'.

**temperament** A horse's or pony's nature, for example, calm, gentle, or excitable.

**top line** The upper part of a horse's back, from the **withers** to the **hindquarters**.

**trot** A **diagonal pace** in which the feet hit the ground in pairs.

**under saddle** When a horse or pony is ridden.

**up to weight** Capable of carrying a heavy rider.

**upright shoulders** Shoulders that do not slope very much from the **withers** to the **point of the shoulder**. They are better for carrying a **harness** collar.

**withers** The bony ridge at the base of a horse's neck.

**zebra marks** Horizontal dark stripes on the legs of primitive breeds of ponies.

# Index

HORSE AND PONY WEB SITES
www.bef.org.uk
(British Equestrian Organization)
www.bhs.org.uk
(official British Horse Society site)
www.equestrian.org
(American horse shows
association – USA equestrian)
www.equiworld.net
(international horse and pony
information)
www.horsesport.org
(Fédération Equestre
Internationale – International
Federation of Equestrian Sport)
www.horseworlddata.com
/breed/html
(general horse and pony
information for enthusiasts)
www.ilph.org
(International League for the
Protection of Horses)
www.imh.org
(International Museum of Horses)
www.pony-club.org.uk
(official Pony Club site)